THE SECOND PENGUIN BOOK
OF ENGLISH MADRIGALS:
FOR FIVE VOICES

DENIS STEVENS, founder-conductor of the Ambrosian Consort and the Accademia Monteverdiana, was educated at Oxford, London, and Paris – combining interests in languages, musicology, and chamber music. He specialized in medieval, Renaissance, and baroque programmes during his five years as a producer in the B.B.C. Music Division, which he left in 1954 for his first visiting professorship in America. After fulfilling invitations to Cornell, Columbia, California (Berkeley), and Pennsylvania State, he became a permanent member of the Department of Music at Columbia University in the City of New York. Dividing his time between research, teaching, and performance, he has made many gramophone records and festival appearances with his musicians, besides editing early music and publishing books such as *A History of Song, Tudor Church Music, Thomas Tomkins,* and (with Alec Robertson) *The Pelican History of Music.* He is also editor of *The Penguin Book of English Madrigals for Four Voices.*

Penguin Books Ltd, Harmondsworth, Middlesex, England
Penguin Books Inc., 7110 Ambassador Road, Baltimore, Maryland 21207, U.S.A.
Penguin Books Australia Ltd, Ringwood, Victoria, Australia

First published 1970

Made and printed in Great Britain by
Halstan & Co. Ltd, Amersham, Bucks.
Set in Monotype Ehrhardt

CONTENTS

EDITORIAL PRINCIPLES

*. . . and likewise you shall be perfectly
understood of the auditor what you sing,
which is one of the highest degrees of
praise which a musician in dittying can
attain unto or wish for.* (Thomas Morley)

A choral group, perhaps, consisting mainly of amateur singers devoted to the madrigal and to comparable vocal forms and styles; or a group of soloists, working together towards great perfection but little reward, other than a purely musical one – no matter what way we hear madrigals performed, the most impressive, delightful, and memorable interpretations are those which breathe spontaneity of a completely natural and unaffected kind. As in so many musics, the art of madrigal singing thrives upon the concealment of art, so that very often the most natural and convincing effects derive from some hidden artifice, whose secret resides in experience, learning, intuition, or an amalgam of all three.

Given a generous allowance of years, experience emerges from practical pursuits, and learning from theoretical; but intuition, born of itself, cannot be commanded to appear, and it is the one ingredient of a fine performance that defies analysis and disarms criticism. Yet there is so much to be absorbed at the lower levels of technical accomplishment that it seems only right, in a brief exposition of editorial methods, to lay more stress upon matters lying nearly within our grasp; and it can hardly be denied that the most useful pre-requisite for a vital re-creation of early music is a text at one and the same time reliable and imaginative.

Music printers in sixteenth-century England were not always reliable, and even when proofs were corrected by unusually careful and conscientious composers, the possibility of error could not be entirely ruled out. But if the great majority of printed madrigals make good musical sense most of the time, the artistic sensibility characteristic of the finest underlay of text to music frequently leaves much to be longed for. Composers relied upon singers to adjust syllables to notes in a manner satisfactory to all concerned. Four hundred years ago, singers were used to such things, just as they were used to part-books bearing only isolated strands of a polyphonic web. Modern singers need scores; and they also need guidance in the matter of text underlay if the original source is at all doubtful or corrupt. These and related topics now call for our attention.

The individual vocal ranges of some Elizabethan madrigals pre-suppose a compass of enviable elasticity resulting perhaps from such social forms of encouragement described in Claude Hollybande's *The French Schoolemaister*, published in 1573:

'Roland, shall we have a song?'

'Yea Sir: where be your books of music? for they be the best corrected.'

'They be in my chest: Katherin, take the key of my closet – you shall find them in a little till at the left hand: behold, there be fair songs at four parts.'

'Who shall sing with me?'

'You shall have company enough: David shall make the bass, John the tenor, and James the treble.'

'Begin! James, take your tune! Go to: for what do you tarry?'

'I have but a rest.'

'Roland, drink afore you begin, you will sing with a better courage.'

'It is well said: give me some white wine – that will cause me to sing better.'

'You must drink some green wine!'

'Yea, truly, to cause me to lose my voice.'

'Oh, see what a funnel, for he hath poured a quart of wine without any taking of his breath.'

Notice that the treble or soprano part is taken not by the lady of the house but by James, probably a choirboy; notice too that the wine-bibber, Roland, is the alto or counter-tenor of this group. By the simple and simultaneous act of whetting his courage and wetting his whistle, he is ready to tackle those low D's more suited to a tenor, or those high E's within the province of a treble.

In the present selection of madrigals, extremes of tessitura have been purposely avoided, so that a normal vocal quartet can be assured of the following ranges:

Ex. 1

It would have been possible to include other works by subjecting them to transposition, but the very sight of a madrigal in the key of B flat minor or F sharp major has been known to strike cheerless chill in the hearts of even the doughtiest singers. Later volumes in this series may experiment along these lines, keeping within the bounds of two flats or two sharps in the key-signature; but for the present purposes non-transposition and medium range have been the guiding principles, and will help to avoid very low notes and very high ones, which Thomas Morley likened respectively to 'a kind of humming' and 'a constrained shrieking'. In some instances, uncomfortable ranges may be avoided by exchanging parts, but the result inevitably alters the tonal balance.

Tonality is such an outstanding characteristic of the madrigalian repertoire that it seems both logical and practical to employ modern key-signatures. Bateson's *And must I needs depart* appears in the original part-books with no key-signature, but the profusion of F sharps and the frequent as well as final cadencing on G tells us that the simplest solution to the problem is the use of a G major key-signature. Ward's *Upon a bank* is just as clearly in G minor, and so the old signature of one flat has been replaced (with, of course, the necessary internal adjustments) by the modern key-signature of two flats. This principle has been followed throughout the volume.

One particular feature of the original part-books has been deliberately and consistently heeded, and that is the exclusion of tempo and dynamic markings. Freshness and spontaneity in performance are sometimes due to a feeling among the singers that they have made a personal contribution to the latent expressive powers of the music, and it is good that they or their director should be able to mould an interpretation after their own ideas, rather than slavishly follow the dynamic droppings of some pedantic editor. One recalls the school hymn written by the Headmaster and set to music by Dr Jolly in Aldous Huxley's *Antic Hay*:

> *(f)* For slack hands and *(dim.)* idle minds
> *(mf)* Mischief still the Tempter finds.
> *(ff)* Keep him captive in his lair;
> *(f)* Work will bind him. *(dim.)* Work is *(pp)* prayer.

Terrace-dynamics of this kind militate against the splendid subtleties of the madrigal and clamp its emotional promise in the strait-jacket of unimaginative reproduction. Let the artists decide for themselves how fast or how slow, how loud or how soft they intend to sing; but let them do so after reading the poem, which is printed here in full before the music begins.

There is, alas, one persuasive and all-pervading characteristic of the part-books that cannot be reproduced – the uninhibited free flow of notes and text without bar lines of any kind. As soon as polyphony is put into score, bar-lines become essential for modern singers and directors, and have in fact been used since the time of the earliest Renaissance scores. Although it is worth remembering that medieval scores disdained bar-lines, relying on rough-and-ready alignment combined with mensural practice to convince singers of their efficacy, a return to this ideal seems out of the question. If modern bar-lines provide welcome orientation, they do so because of their reliability and regularity. Cross-rhythms inherent in the music should not be permitted to dictate fancy barring, except when the shift in stress applies to all voice-parts.

Accordingly, in this edition, barring has been maintained with as much regularity as seems consistent with the style of the music. When individual voice-parts go their own way rhythmically (as they often do) no attempt has been made to mark the music with accents, since these invariably correspond to natural stresses of the verse or of the words themselves. If each poem is read carefully before rehearsal begins, there should be no difficulty in sustaining natural verbal accents at all times and in all voice-parts. For similar reasons, normal tied notes have been preferred to archaic practices involving dots placed to the right of bar-lines. It should not be necessary in this day and age to remind performers that bar-lines do not always coincide with stress or accent. When there is a clear metrical change, however, the nature and extent of this is indicated in order to distinguish between a mensural shift (Tomkins, *Come, shepherds*, bars 14/15) and one that appears as a result of textual accents (Morley, *Cruel, wilt thou persever*, bars 2/3).

Texts have been modernized and punctuated in order to assist interpreters in every possible way, for notwithstanding the variable qualities of English madrigal poetry, the sense of the composition as a whole should emerge clearly in any performance worthy of the name. Capital letters are used to indicate the beginning of a new line in the original poem, since very frequently composers take liberties in setting verse and consequently obscure the underlying structure.

A new feature of this edition will, it is hoped, improve at one and the same time clarity in harmony, declamation, and form. The early part of this introduction hinted at the generally casual attitude towards refinements in both composition and proof-reading as practised in Elizabethan times, and since so many important characteristics of the madrigal are adversely affected by cavalier treatment of this kind, an attempt has been made to incorporate as an editorial method a consistent plan which the present writer has used with success over a number of years.

The first principle is to ensure that musical homophony is matched where appropriate by verbal homophony, all voice-parts singing the same syllables more or less exactly aligned. The more sensitive composers seek this effect as a matter of course, changing the order of words where necessary in order to achieve clarity of declamation.

Repeated phrases, usually shown in the part-books by ditto signs, have been consistently clarified in accordance with this principle of verbal alignment. Occasionally the notes, rather than the words, are out of step in an otherwise regular homophonic pattern, as in Bateson's *Down the hills* (bar 14) where the rhythm of the alto and tenor parts has been adjusted to match that of the other voices.

Another type of adjustment, minor in fact but major in its importance for ease of breathing and accuracy of ensemble, is the regularizing of cadences in so far as the length of their final chord is concerned. In this respect many composers are careful, but not sufficiently so for an entirely satisfactory solution to the problems raised. The original notation of Pilkington's *Sing we, dance we* (bars 13/14) is as follows:

There is no real point, either harmonic or aesthetic, in holding the second soprano and bass G's to the full length of the bar. By reducing them to a minim, the 'z' sound at the end of 'strains' is heard in unison instead of straggling, and the ensuing trio is given a clean start.

Occasionally a note has been clipped for harmonic reasons. There is a passage in Bateson's *Down the hills* where the F sharp (second soprano) and D (alto), if sustained for the written length, would imply a dissonance on the last beat of bar 28. This, being momentary, is certainly not serious; but the abbreviation of the two notes in question allows Bateson's motive to emerge more clearly and to hint rather than point at its harmonic implications.

Ex. 3

A few bars later in the same madrigal, a bass C held to its full length would cause a brief but unresolved dissonance with the change of chord on the fourth beat of bar 32. A dotted minim solves the problem unobtrusively. In the next bar, the alto holds its C for the full bar unnecessarily, since the tenor doubles this note and resolves the seventh chord as one would expect. The alto C has accordingly been shortened to a minim.

Ex. 4

In one instance a repeated final section has been modified as to its point of return, in order to begin a verbal phrase properly rather than start half-way through. This is in Morley's *False love did me inveigle*, where the repeat now accommodates the last two lines of the poem.

It would be pedantic if every single instance of adjustment were made the occasion for a footnote, and in any event the prime purpose of this edition is a practical one. If performers feel that these editorial practices have been carried too far, all they have to do is to lengthen notes that feel uncomfortably short. But I do not think this very likely; and I have never experienced any objection from singers, who are only too willing as a rule to find new and artistic ways to unify breathing, phrasing, and declamation. To the members of my Ambrosian Consort (who have recorded some of these madrigals on HMV Mono HQM 1080 and Stereo HQS 1080) I extend my sincere thanks for many happy years of experiment and co-operation, and if the results as printed here add to the general pleasure of madrigal singing and eventually call for further volumes in this series, my hopes to extend and renew a most delectable form of vocal chamber music will not be in vain.

Columbia University   DENIS STEVENS
In the City of New York
January 1970

I   AND MUST I NEEDS DEPART, THEN?

THOMAS BATESON

> And must I needs depart, then?
> Can pity none come nigh her?
> Farewell, alas, desert then:
> O break asunder, heart, to satisfy her.

Madrigals I à 3, 4, 5, 6 (1604), xiv

Bateson's brief and anonymous lyric has sometimes been compared to an earlier and slightly longer poem, *Now must I part, my dearling*, which Yonge translated from Marenzio's *Parto da voi, mio sole* in the first volume of *Musica Transalpina* (1588). The structure of the text is so faithfully mirrored by the form of the music that no serious problems of interpretation should arise. A moderate tempo is called for, with perhaps a barely perceptible slackening of pace at the third line and a return to *tempo primo* at the fourth. The typical interchange of soprano lines in the second half of the madrigal shows the need for equal status, range, and timbre in these voices, a double echo of a prevailing Italian fashion.

14

19

THOMAS BATESON

Down the hills Corinna trips
Fetching many wanton skips.
To the groves she doth go,
Where thousand birds in a row,
Sitting all upon a tree,
Came two by two and three by three,
Corinna coveting to see,
Tuning notes of her praise,
Do welcome her with roundelays.

Madrigals II à 3, 4, 5, 6 (1618), xiv

Although Bateson's Corinna might be almost any nimble-footed nymph, it is also possible that she represents an up-to-date characterization of the beautiful Greek poetess Corinna, whose prize-winning proclivity was often imputed to her charm rather than to her verse. Pindar, whose work she slighted, called her a Bœotian sow. In any event, Bateson is not really serious, for he sets the opening words to an ascending figure by way of flouting madrigalian convention, then bows to it apologetically in the 'two by two and three by three' passage, which recalls a similar one in *As Vesta was from Latmos hill descending*, by Thomas Weelkes.

3   COME, WOEFUL ORPHEUS

WILLIAM BYRD

Come, woeful Orpheus, with thy charming lyre,
And tune my voice unto thy skilful wire;
Some strange chromatic notes do you devise,
That best with mournful accents sympathize;
Of sourest sharps and uncouth flats make choice,
And I'll thereto compassionate my voice.

Psalmes, Songs, and Sonnets (1611), xix

Sometimes criticized as a parody of madrigal style, or as a vehicle for non-expressive chromatic harmony, this fascinating and (for Byrd) unusual work in fact avoids both madrigalisms and 'eye-music. With commendable honesty, Byrd introduces chromatic notes, sharps, and flats, precisely where the text calls for them, and in so doing he adequately fills the role of the legendary musician by suggesting sorrow and mourning, in harmony with the verse. The greatest care should be exerted to ensure accurate tuning of the 'strange' notes and chords.

best   with   mourn – ful   ac – – – – – cents

mourn – ful   ac – – – cents   do   sym –

That   best   with   mourn – ful   ac – –

That   best____   with   mourn – ful   ac – cents____

That   best   with   mourn – ful   ac – –

40

sym – – – pathe – ize;   Of

___ path – ize,   do   sym – path – ize;____

– cents   sym – path – ize;   Of   sour – est

___ do   sym – – – – path – ize;

– cents   sym – path – ize;   Of   sour – est

45

sour – est   sharps

Of   sour – est   sharps   and   un –

sharps____   make   choice,

Of   sour – est   sharps   and   un – couth   flats,

sharps, of   sour – est   sharps   and   un – couth

4   ZEPHYRUS BRINGS THE TIME

MICHAEL CAVENDISH

Zephyrus brings the time that sweetly scenteth
    With flowers and herbs, and winter's frost exileth;
Progne now chirpeth and Philomel lamenteth,
    Flora the garlands white and red compileth.
Fields do rejoice, the frowning sky relenteth;
    Jove, to behold his dearest daughter, smileth.
The air, the water, the earth to joy consenteth,
    Each creature now to love him reconcileth.

Ayres . . . and Madrigals à 5 (1598), xxii
For his poem, Cavendish takes the octave only of Yonge's happy translation of Petrarch's
Zefiro torna, which appears in settings by Conversi and Ferrabosco in *Musica Transalpina*
(I, 52; II, 2). It was by no means unusual to avoid the more grave sentiments of the sestet by
simply leaving it out, as Watson did in the Marenzio setting contained in his *Italian Madrigals
Englished*, no. 4. Flora, goddess of the flowers, received from Zephyrus her lord and husband
the gift of eternal youth: but the story of Procne and Philomela is less charming by far. A
complex matrimonial problem resulted in their slaying Procne's child and serving its flesh
at the father's dinner-table. The gods in anger transformed Procne into a swallow and Philomela
into a nightingale, ever lamenting their tragedy.

35

43

44

5   WHAT DOTH MY PRETTY DARLING?

MICHAEL EAST

> What doth my pretty darling?
> What doth my song and chanting
> That they sing not of her the praise and vaunting?
> To her I give my violets,
> And garlands sweetly smelling,
> For to crown her sweet locks, pure gold excelling.

Madrigals II à 3, 4, 5 (1606), xx

This is one of several examples of perennial durability in the slightest of madrigal poetry. At some time prior to 1580, an unknown Italian rhymester offered *Che fa oggi il mio sole* to Luca Marenzio, who set it for five voices in his First Book of Madrigals. Yonge translated the text for *Musica Transalpina* (I, 27), which reproduced the Marenzio setting. Several years later, East borrowed the English translation and provided it with new music. In performance, attention should be paid to the repetition of the phrase 'for to crown her sweet locks', since the lower voices tend to sound slightly more ponderous than the preceding trio of high voices.

46

47

6 NOW EACH FLOWERY BANK OF MAY

ORLANDO GIBBONS

Now each flowery bank of May
Woos the streams that glides away;
Mountains fanned by a sweet gale
Loves the humble-looking dale,
Winds the loved leaves do kiss;
Each thing tasteth of love's bliss.
Only I, though blest I be
To be loved by destiny,
Love confessed by her sweet breath,
Whose love is life, whose hate is death.

Madrigals à 5 (1612), xii

If this madrigal, one of the loveliest in Gibbons's only book, is found to lie too high for the tenors, it can be sung a tone lower without inconvenience to the other voices. Its long-sustained lines and flowing polyphony should be respected at all times, even though breathing problems may be considerable. Word-accent and harmonic tension should guide feeling and tempo. If the final note is too long for the soprano, a breath can be taken in bar 85 and the words 'is death' repeated at the same time as the bass.

53

58

59

7   CRUEL, WILT THOU PERSEVER?

THOMAS MORLEY

> Cruel, wilt thou persever
>   Peace to leave ever?
> Peace shalt thou have, and gladness.
>   But when in sadness?
> When thou the morn seest even
>   To fall from heaven.

Canzonets à 5 & 6 (1597), xii
With admirable artistic taste, Morley uses the darker timbre of the SATTB group for the more serious tone of this little dialogue; and he also departs from the usual custom of repeating the first section of a canzonet. It is not the question that is re-stated, but the answer.

63

8   FALSE LOVE DID ME INVEIGLE

THOMAS MORLEY

False love did me inveigle,
And she, like to the eagle,
Upon my breast ay tiring,
Permits me no respiring.

Then would she once but bill me
By the lips, and so kill me!
O but Calisto teareth
My heart out, like the bear whose name she beareth!

Canzonets à 5 & 6 (1597), ii

This insistent young lady, named after one of Diana's not-so-chaste nymphs, is here invested by an unknown poet with avial as well as bestial qualities, the former recalling Shakespeare's vivid account of the queen of love in his *Venus and Adonis* (lines 55–60). Calisto, in ancient legend, was seduced by Jove and gave birth to Arcas, and by the time he had grown up to be a hunter his mother had been changed into a bear by the jealous Juno. Arcas nearly killed Calisto, and the two were thereupon removed to the comparative safety of the heavens, where they continue to shine as the Great and Little Bear. In making his final repeat, Morley missed the sense and syntax of the final couplet, which has here been restored by arranging for the repeat to start a few bars earlier.

NOW IS THE MONTH OF MAYING

THOMAS MORLEY

Now is the month of maying,
When merry lads are playing, fa la,
Each with his bonny lass
Upon the greeny grass. Fa la.

The spring, clad in all gladness,
Doth laugh at winter's sadness, fa la.
And to the bagpipe's sound
The nymphs tread out their ground. Fa la.

Fie then! why sit we musing,
Youth's sweet delight refusing? Fa la.
Say, dainty nymphs, and speak,
Shall we play barley break? Fa la.

Balletts à 5 (1595), iii

One of the most famous of Morley's balletts, this was also arranged for instrumental consort in 1609 by Rosseter (*Lessons for Consort*). In the Italian edition of his 1595 volume, Morley borrowed a text from Vecchi's *Selva di Varia Ricreatione* – 'So ben mi c'ha bon tempo'. But the English version, for more than one reason, is likely to retain its supremacy as long as the art of madrigal singing stays alive.

WERE I A KING

JOHN MUNDY

Were I a king I might command content;
  Were I obscure, unknown should be my cares.
And were I dead, no thoughts should me torment,
  Nor words, nor wrongs, nor loves, nor hopes, nor fears.
A doubtful choice, of three things one to crave,
  A kingdom, or a cottage, or a grave.

Songs and Psalms à 3, 4, 5 (1594), xxvi
Formerly attributed to Edward de Vere, Earl of Oxford, this poem is now known to be the work of the Oxonian playwright William Gager. It is even possible that words and music were written for a play, for the musical texture clearly suggests the uppermost voice as 'the chief singing part' (to borrow a term from Byrd), the four lower parts being assigned to viols. Even in a purely vocal performance it may prove advisable to strive for this impression, by allowing the soprano line its natural prominence, and persuading the other voices to accompany quietly as if they constituted a separate but closely related group.

me tor - ment, Nor words, nor words, nor

____ tor - ment, Nor words, nor

me tor - ment, Nor words, nor

me tor - ment, Nor words, nor

me tor - ment, Nor words, nor

wrongs, nor wrongs, nor loves, nor

words, nor wrongs, nor wrongs, nor loves,

words, nor wrongs, nor wrongs, nor loves,

words, nor wrongs, nor wrongs, nor loves,

words, nor wrongs, nor wrongs, nor loves,

loves, nor hopes, nor fears. A

nor loves, nor hopes,____ nor ____ fears. A

nor loves, nor hopes, nor fears. A

nor loves, nor ____ hopes, nor fears.

nor loves, nor hopes, nor fears.

II   SING WE, DANCE WE ON THE GREEN

FRANCIS PILKINGTON

Sing we, dance we on the green,
And fill these valleys with our melodious strains,
For joy that our summer's queen,
Environed with all the country swains,
Fairly trips it o'er the plains.
Let us about these daffadillies sweet
Tread a ring-dance with our feet.

Madrigals and Pastorals à 3, 4, 5 (1613), xvi
The prevailing homophony and dance-like lilt of this charming madrigal call for the utmost lightness and precision in performance. Note that the Chester cleric does not approve of interchanged sopranos on the final repeat.

83

40

trips it o'er the plains. Let us a - bout, let us a -

trips it o'er the plains. Let us a - bout, let us a -

o'er the plains. Let us a - bout, let us a -

trips it o'er the plains. Let us a - bout, let us a -

trips it o'er the plains. Let us a - bout, let us a -

- bout these daf - fa - dil - lies sweet,

- bout these daf - fa - dil - lies sweet,

- bout these daf - fa - dil - lies sweet, let us a -

- bout, let us a - bout these

- bout, let us a - bout these

these daf - fa - dil - lies

a - bout these daf - fa - dil - lies sweet,

- bout these daf - fa - dil - lies sweet,

daf - fa - dil - lies sweet, these

daf - fa - dil - lies sweet, let us a - bout these

12 COME, SHEPHERDS, SING WITH ME

THOMAS TOMKINS

Come, shepherds, sing with me.
Thrice happy might we be
If we should never see
Love and his misery. Fa la.

Love, now we hate thy lore,
More than we loved before.
From hence we all have swore
To love false Love no more. Fa la.

Songs à 3, 4, 5, 6 (1622), xv
Dedicated to Nathaniel Giles, organist of Worcester Cathedral and later of St George's Chapel, Windsor. The opening chorus of shepherdesses can be as persuasive as required, though not without a touch of humour: at the words 'Thrice happy might we be', Tomkins retains the trio as well as changing the time to a cheerful tripla. The fa-la section is one of the longest of its kind, and it needs careful shaping and perfect control over stress and texture.

la la la la, fa la la la la la
fa la la la la la la, fa la la
la, fa la la la la, fa la la la,
fa la la la la la la, fa la,
la la la, fa la la la la la la,

la, fa la la la la la
la la la la la, fa la la
fa la la la la, fa la la la, fa la la
fa la la la la la la la,
fa la la la la la la la, fa

la, fa la la. Love, now we hate thy
la la la la. Love, now we hate thy
la la la la. Love, now we hate thy___
fa la la la. Love, now we hate thy
la la la la.

94

TO THE SHADY WOODS

THOMAS TOMKINS

To the shady woods now wend we,
And there the mid-day spend we. Fa la.
There Phoebus' self is colder,
And we may be the bolder. Fa la.

Songs à 3, 4, 5, 6 (1622), xiii
Tomkins dedicated this madrigal to his friend Robert Chetwode, and the opening line of the poem may perhaps be a pun on his name. That this was by no means unusual is shown by the first of Monteverdi's canzonets (Venice, 1584), which mentions 'Ambrosia dolce, tanto delicata'. The name of the dedicatee was Pietro Ambrosini.

99

14　AH SWEET, WHOSE BEAUTY

THOMAS VAUTOR

Ah sweet, whose beauty passeth all my telling,
To thee my love all others are excelling. Fa la.
By thee I live and have my only pleasure,
Thou art my life and eke my whole heart's treasure. Fa la.

Let not unkindness then eclipse my gladness,
But let sweet smiles expel the clouds of sadness. Fa la.
For if my love sweet looks and liking reapeth,
O happy I, my heart for joy it leapeth. Fa la.

Songs of Divers Airs and Natures (1619), iii
The optimistic and outgoing nature of the lyric, combined with the presence of a fa-la refrain,
should not be taken as an indication of an immoderately fast tempo.

-cell - ing, all o - thers — are ex - cell - ing.
trea - sure, and eke — my — whole heart's trea - sure.

-cell - ing, all o - thers — are ex - cell - ing.
trea - sure, and eke — my — whole heart's trea - sure.

are _____ ex - cell - ing, are ex - cell - -
eke — my — whole heart's, eke my whole heart's trea - - -

o - thers are all o - thers are ex - cell - ing. Fa la
eke — my — whole heart's, eke my whole heart's trea sure.

o - - thers are ex - cell - - -
eke my whole heart's trea - - -

— Fa la la, fa la la la la, fa la la la la, fa la la la la

— Fa la la la la la la, fa la la la la la la, fa la la la la

-ing.
-sure. Fa _____ la la la, fa la la la la la la

-ing.
-sure. la la la la, fa la la la la

-ing. Fa la la la la la la la la, fa la la la
-sure.

glad - ness, But let sweet smiles ex - pel the clouds of
reap - eth, O hap - py I, my heart for joy it

glad - ness, But let sweet smiles ex - pel the clouds of
reap - eth, O hap - py I, my heart for joy it

— But let sweet smiles ex - pel the clouds of
— O hap - py I, my heart for joy it

glad - ness, But let sweet smiles ex - pel the clouds of
reap - eth, O hap - py I, my heart for joy it

glad - ness, But let sweet smiles ex - pel the clouds of
reap - eth, O hap - py I, my heart for joy it

sad - ness. Fa la la la, fa la la la, fa
leap - eth.

sad - ness. Fa la la la, fa la la la, fa
leap - eth.

sad - ness. Fa la la la la la la la, fa la la la
leap - eth.

sad - ness. Fa la la la la la, fa la la la la la
leap - eth.

sad - ness. Fa la la
leap - eth.

15　MOTHER, I WILL HAVE A HUSBAND

THOMAS VAUTOR

Mother, I will have a husband,
And I will have him out of hand.
　Mother, I will sure have one,
　In spite of her that will have none.

John a Dun should have had me long ere this,
He said I had good lips to kiss.
　Mother, I will sure have one,
　In spite of her that will have none.

For I have heard 'tis trim when folks do love,
By good Sir John I swear now I will prove.
　For, Mother, I will sure have one,
　In spite of her that will have none.

To the town therefore will I gad,
To get me a husband good or bad.

Mother, I will have a husband,
And I will have him out of hand.
　Mother, I will sure have one,
　In spite of her that will have none.

Songs of Divers Airs and Natures (1619), iv
The tempo-relationship between the main section and the tripla (bars 39/40) is made clear by
the first two entries of 'To the town therefore will I gad'. Natural word-stress dictates the
hemiola pattern until bar 48.

have him out of hand. Mo-ther, I will sure have

have him out of hand. Mo-ther, I will sure have

have him out of hand. Mo-ther, I will sure have

have him out of ____ hand. Mo-ther, I will sure have

have him out of hand. Mo-ther, I will sure have

one, have one, In spite of her, of her that will have

one, have one, In spite of her, of her that will have

one, In spite of her, of her that will have

one, In spite of ____ her, of ____ her ____ that will have

one, In spite of her, of her that will have

none. John a Dun should have had me long ere this, John a

none. John a Dun should have had me long ere this, John a

none. John a Dun should have had me long ere this, John a

none. John a

none. John a

For, Mo-ther, I will sure have one, have

For, Mo-ther, I will sure have one, have

Mo-ther, I will sure have one, have one, have

Mo-ther, I will sure have one, have one, have

Mo-ther, I will sure have one, have one, have

one, have one, In spite of her that will have none.

one, have one, In spite of her that will have none.

one, have one, In spite of her that will have none.

one, have one, In spite of her that will have none.

one, have one, In spite of her that will have none.

To the town there-fore will I

To the town there-fore will I gad, to the

To the town there-fore will I gad, will I gad, will I

To the town there-fore will I gad, will I gad, will I

To the town there-fore will I gad,

UPON A BANK

JOHN WARD

Upon a bank with roses set about,
   Where pretty turtles, joining bill to bill,
And gentle springs steal softly murmuring out,
   Washing the foot of pleasure's sacred hill;
     There little Love sore wounded lies,
   His bow and arrows broken,
     Bedewed with tears from Venus' eyes;
   O grievous to be spoken!

Madrigals à 3, 4, 5, 6 (1613), xviii
Michael Drayton's poem first appeared as 'Near to a bank . . . ' in *England's Helicon* (1600);
the later form, which Ward adopted, comes from the second eclogue of Drayton's *Poems
Lyric and Pastoral* (1606). The perfect partnership of poetry and music deserves a performance
full of subtlety, care, and sensitivity to the declamation.

17 COLD WINTER'S ICE IS FLED

THOMAS WEELKES

Cold winter's ice is fled and gone,
    And summer brags on every tree;
The redbreast peeps amidst the throng
    Of wood-born birds that wanton be.
Each one forgets what they have been,
And so doth Phyllis, summer's queen.

Madrigals à 5 & 6 (1600), i

The opening bars in particular should be carefully tuned because they show so clearly the composer's reaction to the meaning of the word 'cold' within its warmer phrase: minor gives way to major, quite deliberately and unequivocally.

been, what they have been,

been, what they have been,

been, what they have been, Each one for-gets what

Each one for - gets what they

Each one for - gets what

And so doth Phyl - lis, sum -

And so doth Phyl - lis,

they have been, have been, And so doth

have __ been, what they have been,

they have __ been, what they have been,

- mer's __ queen, __

sum - mer's __ queen, __ sum -

Phyl - lis, sum - mer's __ queen, and so doth

And so doth Phyl - lis, sum -

And so doth Phyl - lis, sum -

SING WE AT PLEASURE

THOMAS WEELKES

Sing we at pleasure,
Content is our treasure. Fa la.
Sweet Love shall keep the ground,
Whilst we his praises sound.
All shepherds in a ring
Shall, dancing, ever sing: Fa la.

Balletts and Madrigals à 5 & 6 (1598), xii

The 'ground' kept by Love was presumably one of the standard harmonic patterns used throughout the sixteenth and seventeenth centuries as a basis for improvisation. Weelkes does not actually quote one, but the movement of his bass part where these words occur seems to hint at the melodic leaps which characterize the majority of grounds.

-tent is our trea - sure, con - tent is our trea - sure.

trea - sure, con - tent is our trea - sure.

trea - sure, con - tent is our trea - sure, trea - sure. Fa

trea - sure, con - tent is our trea - sure, our trea - sure. Fa

- tent is our trea - sure, con - tent is our trea - sure. Fa

Fa la la la la,

Fa la la la la la la la la

la la la la la la la la la la la la la

la la la la la la la la la, fa la

la la la la la la, fa la la la

fa la la la la la la la la la

la la la la, fa la la la

la la la la la la la, fa la la la

la la la la la la la la la la la la

la la la la la la la la la

135

19   FLORA GAVE ME FAIREST FLOWERS

JOHN WILBYE

Flora gave me fairest flowers,
  None so fair in Flora's treasure.
These I placed on Phyllis' bowers,
  She was pleased, and she my pleasure.
Smiling meadows seem to say:
Come, ye wantons, here to play.

Madrigals I à 3, 4, 5, 6 (1598), xxii
When a feminine ending corresponds, as it does so often, to a musical cadence or half-close, it is worth while taking care to reproduce the word-accents in the music, naturally at the expense of the modern bar-line, which is nothing more than a guide.

20

OFT HAVE I VOWED

JOHN WILBYE

Oft have I vowed how dearly I did love thee,
   And oft observed thee with all willing duty.
Sighs I have sent, still hoping to remove thee;
   Millions of tears I tendered to thy beauty.

Yet thou, of sighs and silly tears regardless,
   Suff'rest my feeble heart to pine with anguish,
Whilst all my barren hopes return rewardless,
   My bitter days do waste and I do languish.

Madrigals II à 3, 4, 5, 6 (1609), xx

At the second appearance of the word 'sighs' (line 5 of the poem), Wilbye resorts to the musical meaning of the word – a crotchet rest. This effect delighted Henry Peacham, who mentions it in connexion with a madrigal by Vecchi: 'Again, in *S'io potessi raccor' i miei sospiri*, the breaking of the word *sospiri* with crotchet and crotchet-rest into sighs . . . ' (*The Compleat Gentleman*, 1622).

ten - dered to thy beau - - -

- lions of tears I ten - dered to thy beau -

beau - ty, mil - lions of tears I ten - dered to thy

- lions of tears I ten - dered to thy beau - -

thy beau - - - -

35

- ty. Yet thou, of sighs and sil - ly tears re -

- ty. Yet thou, of sighs and sil - ly tears re -

beau - ty. Yet thou, of sighs and sil - ly tears re -

- ty.

- ty.

40

-gard - less, yet thou, of sighs and

-gard - less, yet thou, of sighs and

-gard - less, yet thou, of sighs, yet thou of

Yet thou, of sighs and

Yet thou, of sighs and

sil - ly tears re - gard - less,

sil - ly tears re - gard - less,

sighs and sil - ly tears re - gard - less,

sil ly tears re - gard - less, Suff - 'rest my

sil - ly tears re - gard - less, Suff - 'rest my

45

Suff - 'rest my fee - ble heart, my fee - ble

Suff - 'rest my_____ fee -

fee - ble_____ heart,

fee - ble heart, my fee - ble heart to pine

50

Suff - 'rest my fee - ble heart, to pine_____

heart to pine with an - guish, with an - -

- ble heart to_____ pine

suff - 'rest my

with an - guish, to_____

149

all my bar-ren hopes re-turn,_____ re-ward — —

all my bar-ren hopes re-turn,_____ re-ward — —

all my bar — ren hopes_____

— — less,_____

— — less, My bit-ter days do waste and

My bit-ter days_____ do

_____ re-turn, re-ward — less, My bit-ter

My bit-ter

My bit-ter days

I do lan — guish, my bit-ter

waste and I do lan-guish, my

days do_____ waste and_____ I do

days do — waste and I

150

21

WEEP, WEEP, MINE EYES

JOHN WILBYE

Weep, weep, mine eyes, my heart can take no rest,
Weep, weep, my heart, mine eyes shall ne'er be blest.
Weep eyes, weep heart, and both this accent cry:
A thousand deaths, Flamminia, I die.

Ay me, ah cruel Fortune! Now, Leander, to die I fear not.
  Death, do thy worst, I care not!
I hope when I am dead in Elysian plain
To meet, and there with joy we'll love again.

Madrigals II à 3, 4, 5, 6 (1609), xxiii
Perhaps this passionate dialogue comes from a play performed when Wilbye lived at Hengrave Hall. The name Flamminia is unusual, especially in partnership with Leander, though the Italian poem used throughout the collection *L'Amorosa Ero* (1588) associates Hero with Narcissus.

153

Now,_____ Le - an - der, to die I fear

Now,_____ Le - an - der,_____ to die

me! Now,_____ Le - an - der, to die_____ I

Now,_____ Le - an - der,_____ to

not. Death, do thy worst, I care

I fear_____ not. Death, do thy

fear_____ not. Death, do thy

die_____ I fear not. Death, do thy

not, Death, do thy worst, I care_____ not, Death,

worst, I care_____ not, Death, do thy worst, I care_____

worst, I_____ care_____ not, Death, do thy

worst, I care_____ not, Death, do thy worst, I_____

Death, do thy worst, I care_____ not, Death,